Contents

Why should I look after my teeth?

You need your teeth to eat food.

Your teeth get plaque on them
after you eat.

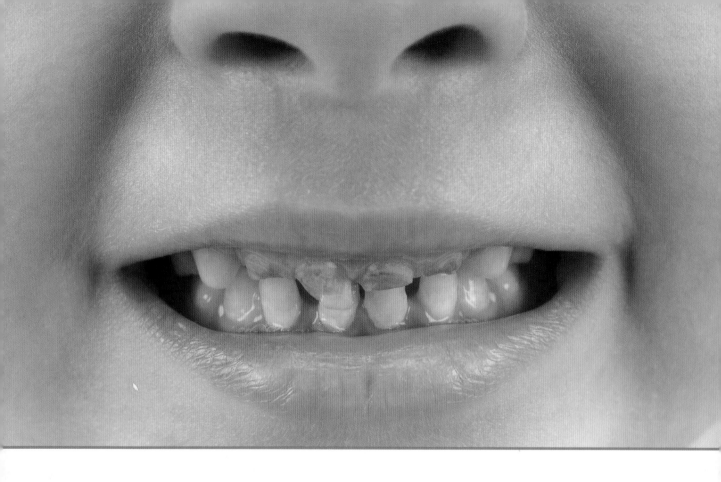

Plaque makes teeth go bad.

This makes your teeth hurt.

How to brush your teeth

When you brush your teeth
you get rid of the plaque.

Put a pea-sized bit of toothpaste
on your brush.

Brush around every tooth.

Brush the hard to reach
places, too.

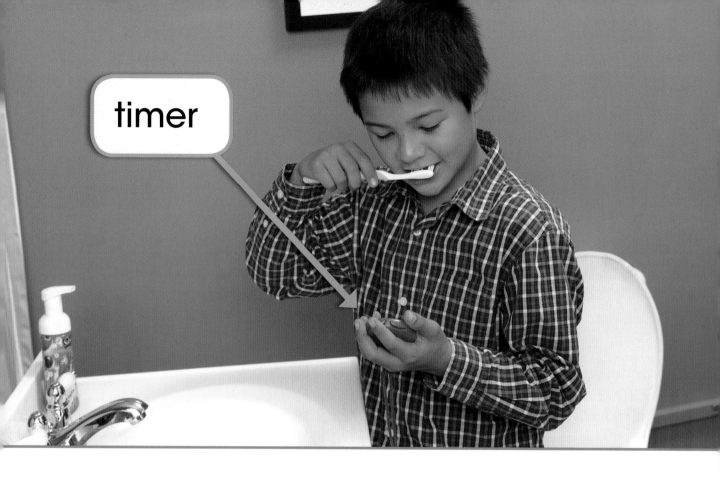

timer

Brush for about two minutes.

You could use a timer to help you.

12

Spit the toothpaste out in the sink.

When should I brush my teeth?

Brush your teeth after breakfast.

Brush your teeth before you sleep.

Brush your teeth after lunch
or snacks if you can.

Other ways to look after your teeth

You can drink water at any time.

Water is not bad for your teeth.

Sweets are bad for your teeth.
Sugary drinks are bad for your teeth.

Try not to have sweet things very often.

Brush your teeth afterwards
if you can.

You should see the dentist
twice a year.

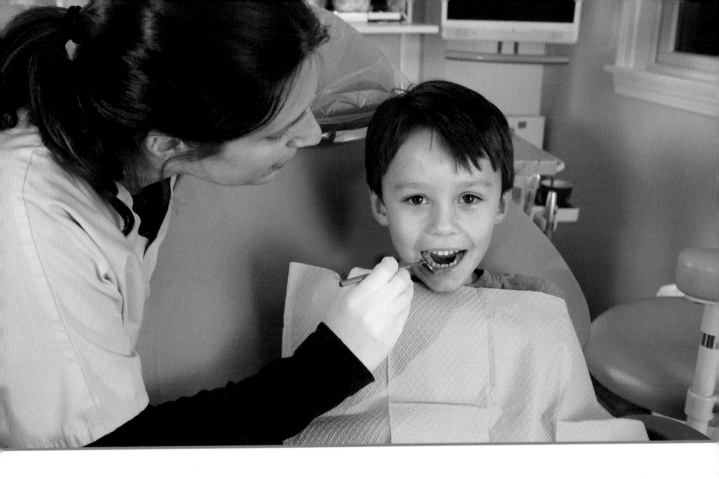

The dentist will check to see if your
teeth are clean and healthy.

Can you remember?

When should you brush your teeth?

Answer on page 24

Picture glossary

 **dentist** doctor who looks after people's teeth

 **plaque** something you get on your teeth after you eat or drink. You cannot see plaque but it is bad for your teeth.

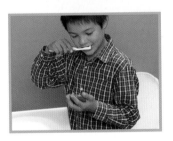 **timer** machine a bit like a clock. A timer can tell you how long it takes to do something.

Index

Answer to question on page 22
You need to brush your teeth after breakfast and before you go to bed.
You should also brush your teeth after eating lunch, snacks, or sweet things if you can.

Notes for parents and teachers

Before reading
Ask the children why we need teeth. Find out what they know about how to take care of their teeth and record their ideas. Read the book to see where these ideas overlap.

After reading
- If possible, ask a dentist or hygienist to speak to the children about what they need to do to take care of their teeth. Use a toothbrush, model of teeth, and a timer and ask a child to brush the teeth for 2 minutes. Which teeth were harder to clean? Demonstrate how to brush your teeth well.

- Draw a face with an open, smiling mouth (crescent shaped). Give the children a quiz on how to look after their teeth. For each question they get right add a tooth to the mouth. Can they collect a full set of teeth?